JUN   2009

DATE DUE

D1274418

SUPER SANDCASTLE
State Stories

THE LONESOME STAR

~ A Story About Texas ~

Written by Karen Latchana Kenney

Illustrated by Bob Doucet

Consulting Editor, Diane Craig, M.A./Reading Specialist

ABDO
Publishing Company

Published by ABDO Publishing Company
8000 West 78th Street, Edina, Minnesota 55439.

Editor: Pam Price
Content Developer: Nancy Tuminelly
Cover and Interior Design and Production:
   Anders Hanson, Mighty Media
Photo Credits: Shutterstock

Library of Congress Cataloging-in-Publication Data

Kenney, Karen Latchana.
  The lonesome star : a story about Texas / Karen Latchana
Kenney ; Illustrated by Bob Doucet.
     p. cm. -- (Fact & fable. State stories)
  ISBN 978-1-60453-184-8
  1. Texas--Juvenile literature. I. Doucet, Bob, ill. II. Title.

  F386.3.K46 2009
  976.4--dc22
                            2008007206

Super SandCastle™ books are created by a team of
professional educators, reading specialists, and content
developers around five essential components—phonemic
awareness, phonics, vocabulary, text comprehension,
and fluency—to assist young readers as they develop
reading skills and strategies and increase their general
knowledge. All books are written, reviewed, and leveled
for guided reading, early reading intervention, and
Accelerated Reader® programs for use in shared, guided,
and independent reading and writing activities to
support a balanced approach to literacy instruction.

TABLE OF CONTENTS

mockingbird (pg. 8)

Red River

Lubbock

rodeo (pg. 17)

Fort Worth

Guadalupe Peak (pg. 13)

Dallas (pg. 16)

El Paso

Texas longhorn (pg. 14)

cotton (pg. 15)

bluebonnet (pg. 7)

Austin (pg. 6)

TEXAS

Houston

nine-banded armadillo (pg. 5)

Rio Grande

San Antonio

prickly pear cactus (pg. 9)

Corpus Christi

LEGEND

☆ CAPITAL

● STORY START

○ CITY

- - - STORY PATH

⋀⋀ MOUNTAINS

✖ STORY END

〰 RIVER

THE LONESOME STAR

Far above the tall pecan trees of Texas, way beyond the clouds, lived a little star named Sam. One day, a bright comet crossed his path. BOOM! The crash sent Sam spinning through space, and he fell to Earth.

THUD! "Ouch!" cried Sam as he landed on a rock. He looked around, but nothing looked familiar. "Where am I?" Sam asked aloud.

Suddenly, the rock moved, and Sam noticed it had a narrow head with pointy ears and beady eyes. "You are in Texas!" it said.

"Yikes! What are you?" Sam asked.

"I'm an armadillo named Annie," she answered. "So what are you?"

Nine-Banded Armadillo

The nine-banded armadillo is the official small animal of Texas. It has a bony shell-like body, a long tail, and strong claws.

Austin, Texas

Austin is the capital of Texas. It is the fourth-largest city in Texas. The state capitol building is the tallest and largest state capitol building in the United States.

"My name is Sam," he replied. "I'm a star, and I want to go back home!"

Annie remembered her friend talking about stars just the other day. She said, "I heard there are stars at the rodeo in Austin. Maybe they can help you. It's a long way, so let's get going!"

Sam and Annie walked along the riverbank. Soon they came to a sea of beautiful blue flowers. Butterflies and birds fluttered between the flowers and the sky. "Oh, Annie," Sam yelled, "this is amazing!"

Bluebonnet

The bluebonnet is the Texas state flower. This bright blue flower with white tips grows about 12 inches high.

Mockingbird

The mockingbird is the Texas state bird. Mockingbirds copy, or mock, other birdcalls and repeat them quickly two or three times.

"This is amazing. This is amazing," shrieked a voice.

"Who is that?" Sam inquired.

Annie whispered, "It's a mockingbird. It will repeat everything you say."

The bird flew down and said, "Hi! My name's Molly. What's going on?"

"We're going to the rodeo," Annie replied. "Want to come?"

Molly shouted, "Yes! Yes!"

Prickly Pear

The prickly pear cactus is the official Texas state plant. It is found in the desert regions of Texas. This cactus has both large, sharp spines and smaller, soft spines that protect the plant.

The land became rocky as the three started going uphill. Sam tripped and almost fell. "Sam, be careful! Those prickly pears have spines that really hurt if they stick you! I'll carry you for a while," Annie said.

"Thank you!" Sam said gratefully.

"Thank you! Thank you!" repeated Molly.

Jalapeño Pepper

The jalapeño is the Texas state pepper. Texas is the largest grower of jalapeño peppers in the United States.

Sam rode on Annie's back into a beautiful red sunset that quickly turned dark. Millions of sparkles twinkled in the night sky. Annie felt drips on her back and said, "Don't cry, Sam."

Sam sniffled, "Sorry, I just miss my friends."

"Molly and I are your friends!" Annie answered.

Molly flew ahead when she saw a campfire. "Hello. Hello. I'm Molly!" she screeched.

"Howdy, Molly! This is Wild Chili Willie, and I'm Panhandle Hank. Bring your friends over and have some of Willie's mighty fine chili," invited Hank.

"This old family recipe is pretty mild. If you like hot food, just add some of these jalapeño peppers!" Willie said as he smiled.

Chili

Chili became the state dish of Texas in 1977. There are many chili recipes that use different kinds of meats, beans, and spices.

Willie's Mighty Fine Chili

2 tablespoons oil

1 large onion, peeled and chopped

1 1/4 pounds fresh ground turkey

2 large cloves garlic, peeled and minced

2 teaspoons chili powder

1/2 teaspoon ground black pepper

1/2 teaspoon salt

1/2 teaspoon ground cumin

1 can (15 ounces) pinto beans

1 can (14 1/2-ounces) diced tomatoes with the juice

1 can (14 1/2-ounces) chicken broth

Ask an adult for help cutting and cooking the food. Heat the oil in a pan over medium heat for 1 minute. Add the onion and cook until it is soft. Add the turkey and garlic and brown them for 5 minutes. Add the chili powder, pepper, salt, cumin, beans, tomatoes, and broth. Simmer the chili for 15 minutes. Serve with chopped green onions and sour cream.

Makes 8 one-cup servings.

Hank asked, "Where y'all going?"

"We're going to the rodeo," Sam answered.

"That's where we're headed!" Willie hollered. Hank sang and played his guitar while the others drifted off to sleep. Sam dreamed that he, Annie, and Molly were back home with his friends.

Cowboys

Cowboys ride horses, herd cattle, and compete in rodeos in Texas and other western states. They wear big hats, boots, and blue jeans. Sometimes they wear chaps.

12

Guadalupe Peak

Guadalupe Peak is located in Guadalupe Mountains National Park. It is the highest point in Texas. It rises 8,749 feet above sea level.

The sun rose over Guadalupe Peak. Hank and Willie got up and packed their wagon. They hitched the wagon to one of the horses. "Rise and shine, little critters," Hank called. Sam, Annie, and Molly climbed sleepily into the wagon. The cowboys shouted, "Giddyap!" and off they went.

Texas Longhorn

The Texas longhorn is the state large animal. They have horns that can grow up to six feet long, measured tip to tip.

As the wagon bounced along, Sam looked around. He saw huge creatures with very long horns feeding in the grasslands. MOOO. "What are those?" he asked Annie.

Annie laughed as she answered, "Longhorn cattle. You will see them at the rodeo too!"

Farther down the road, white balls filled the fields. "What's that?" Sam inquired.

"It's cotton. Clothes are made from it," Annie explained. Then they passed a sign that read Dallas 10 miles. Annie yelled, "Hey, I thought we were going to Austin!"

"Nope, Dallas or bust!" Hank and Willie replied. "Best rodeo this side of the Rio Grande!"

"Oh well," Annie said to Sam, "a rodeo is a rodeo!"

Cotton

Cotton is the official state fiber and cloth of Texas. Texas produces more cotton than any other state.

Soon Hank shouted, "We're in Dallas!" They rode through a gate with a big sign that said Championship Rodeo. Hank and Willie tied their horses to a post. "Follow us!" they said. People were crowded around a big ring.

"I wonder where the stars are," Sam thought.

Dallas

Dallas is the third-largest city in Texas and the ninth largest in the United States. Its nicknames are D-Town and Big D. Its slogan is "Live Large. Think Big."

The crowd cheered as a cowboy riding a wild bucking bull charged into the ring. "That's Rompin' Rex, the biggest rodeo star in Texas!" Hank exclaimed.

"He's a star?" Sam asked.

"Oh, Sam," Annie cried, "rodeo stars are people, not actual stars! I'm so sorry. Now how will you get back home to your friends?"

Rodeo

Rodeo comes from Mexico. Today it is a popular sport in Texas. Rodeo events include bull riding, cattle wrestling, barrel racing, and team roping.

17

Square Dance

The state dance of Texas is the square dance. Four couples form a square and move together to directions shouted out by a "caller." Square dance music is played on banjos, fiddles, accordions, and guitars.

Before Sam could reply, a loudspeaker announced, "Square dance competition in five minutes!"

"Oh, this will be fun. Come on. Come on!" said Molly. They watched brightly dressed couples swinging their partners to lively music.

"That does look like fun!" giggled Sam. "Can we try it?" They twirled each other around until they were dizzy.

Sam said, "I'm not feeling so lonely anymore. Having you two as friends makes me feel like I am home."

"Let's enjoy the rodeo and decide what to do tomorrow," said Annie. "Who knows, maybe we will find some more friends!"

"Friends. Friends," repeated Molly.

THE END

Friendship

Friendship is the state motto of Texas. The name Texas originally came from the Caddo Indian word *teysha*, which means "hello, friend."

TEXAS AT A GLANCE

Abbreviation:
TX

Capital:
Austin

Largest city: Houston
(4th-largest U.S. city)

Statehood: December
29, 1845 (28th state)

Area:
268,581 sq. mi.
(695,622 sq km)
(2nd-largest state)

Nickname:
Lone Star State

Motto:
friendship

State bird: mockingbird

State flower: bluebonnet

State tree: pecan

State mammal: armadillo

State insect:
monarch butterfly

State song:
"Texas, Our Texas"

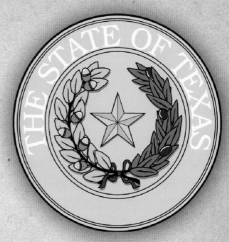

STATE SEAL

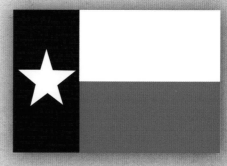

STATE FLAG

STATE QUARTER

The Texas quarter has the state outline and a star on the back. This represents the state nickname, the Lone Star State. The rope around the edge stands for cattle and cowboys.

WHAT DO YOU KNOW?

How well do you remember the story? Match the pictures to the questions below. Then check your answers at the bottom of the page.

a. armadillo

b. bull

c. mockingbird

d. rodeo

e. prickly pear cactus

f. Texas longhorn

1. What kind of creature is Annie?

2. What kind of animal is Molly?

3. What did Annie tell Sam to be careful of?

4. When he was riding in the wagon, what kind of animal did Sam see?

5. What did Sam, Annie, and Molly go to Dallas to see?

6. What did Rompin' Rex ride?

WHAT TO DO IN TEXAS

1 VISIT NASA
Johnson Space Center in Houston

2 GO TO A BEACH
Padre Island National Seashore

3 SEE AN OLD MISSION
The Alamo in San Antonio

4 EXPLORE NATURE
Enchanted Rock State Natural Area north of Fredericksburg

5 VISIT A NATIONAL PARK
Big Bend National Park near Terlingua

6 LEARN ABOUT PRAIRIE DOGS
Prairie Dog Town in Lubbock

7 EXPERIENCE MODERN ART
The Modern Art Museum of Fort Worth

8 SEE A BIG CITY FROM ABOVE
Observation deck of Reunion Tower in Dallas